Praise for *Mama Phife Represents*

"A teacher begets a teacher and a poet begets a poet. This book is the embodiment of pure love, grace, and hope. Herein, Mama Phife, aka Cheryl Boyce-Taylor, has given us a gift about her greatest gift, her son Malik "Phife Dawg" Taylor. Malik was a great storyteller. To say he got it from his mama is an understatement. He was a treasure to me and Cheryl's writings and memoirs help to comfort the place that misses him greatly. I thank her for this book and for still teaching us . . . like her mother before her."

—ALI SHAHEED MUHAMMAD, A Tribe Called Quest

"I am eternally hopeful that more people in the world come to terms with understanding that for anyone to share an experience of grief is a true generosity. With *Mama Phife Represents*, Cheryl Boyce-Taylor allows a reader to bask in the generosity. The sharing of loss and grief is the building of a bridge that others who have experienced that specific loss can cross. This is a book about losing a child, yes. But beyond that, it is a book of tactile emotions, and a singularly musical writing, which Boyce-Taylor has always done so well. Above all, *Mama Phife Represents* shows anyone who has lost someone how to make the most of memory, and the most of their own survival."

—HANIF ABDURRAQIB, author of *Go Ahead in the Rain:*
Notes to A Tribe Called Quest

"'All around are unhinged bones / wailing at the lip of sea.' And: 'I've stitched your breath / to my throat.' Such lines carry the loss of the writer's beautiful son out of which emerges this book of love, of joy, of grief, but also of plenty. Through poems, letters, photographs, and other communications, Cheryl Boyce-Taylor has gathered an exquisite record of this great love between mother and son, artist and artist. Quietly I say to you here: It is like nothing else I have read. An elegy, an epic, a duet. A motherhand gathering the lastings. We are so utterly fortunate to witness this immense devotion, and in that witnessing be changed by yet another glimpse of deepest love and what it makes possible."

—ARACELIS GIRMAY, author of *The Black Maria*

"Malik Phife Dawg Taylor represents everything that's beautiful about hip-hop. I had the honor of meeting his mother Cheryl Boyce-Taylor, the poet, long before I met him. She inspired me to become a better artist. When I became a professional artist, Malik was one of my biggest supporters. Without them, I don't know if I would be the artist I am today. This book is like a piece of me."

—TALIB KWELI, hip-hop artist

"*Mama Phife Represents* is an intimate and heartbreaking tribute to Boyce-Taylor's son, Malik 'Phife Dawg' Taylor. Not only does Boyce-Taylor deftly humanize the hip-hop superhero, but she also logs every fragile emotion in both eulogy and celebration: so much so that 'she will travel to Anguilla / beg Yemaya to bring him back.' The light that the poet finds on this journey is nearly unfathomable, but always redemptive. This collection is a monument, and I am grateful for it."

—MICHAEL CIRELLI, CEO of Urban Word
National Youth Poet Laureate Program

"*Mama Phife Represents* is at once a memoir and a living archive of one man's extraordinary life and his mother's love and pain in the face of his loss. At a time in the United States when so many Black mothers are losing their Black children—through illness and violence—this book stands as a testament to the deep, ground-shifting impact of that loss across generations. Honest, healing, timely."

—DR. ANA-MAURINE LARA, poet, novelist, and scholar

"These poems shred and rebuild. They keen and holler, they are not ashamed. Not afraid. They drill hard to the marrow of suffering and rise up alive. Singing. A mourning song, yes, but a song. It is sometimes 'the crude voice of earth's sorrow,' but it also, and always, unmistakably and unshakably Cheryl's. The poet, the mother, the wife, the lover, singing into her own, and by extension the world's survival and renewal and re-blooming. If we are lucky, someday someone will say of each of us when we are lost, 'all the stars have followed after you.'"

—MARTY MCCONNELL, author of *when they say you can't go home again, what they mean is you were never there*

THE BREAKBEAT POETS SERIES

The BreakBeat Poets series, created by Kevin Coval and Nate Marshall, is committed to work that brings the aesthetic of hip-hop practice to the page. These books are a cipher for the fresh, with an eye always to the next. We strive to center and showcase some of the most exciting voices in literature, art, and culture.

THE BREAKBEAT POETS EDITORIAL BOARD
Cofounders Kevin Coval (Creative Director) and Nate Marshall (Series Editor), Maya Marshall (Managing Editor), Safia Elhillo, Idris Goodwin, and José Olivarez

BREAKBEAT POETS SERIES TITLES INCLUDE
The BreakBeat Poets Vol. 1: New American Poetry in the Age of Hip-Hop
edited by Kevin Coval, Quraysh Ali Lansana, and Nate Marshall
This is Modern Art: A Play by Idris Goodwin and Kevin Coval
The BreakBeat Poets Vol. 2: Black Girl Magic
edited by Mahogany L. Browne, Jamila Woods, and Idrissa Simmonds
Human Highlight by Idris Goodwin and Kevin Coval
On My Way to Liberation by H. Melt
Black Queer Hoe by Britteney Black Rose Kapri
Citizen Illegal by José Olivarez
Graphite by Patricia Frazier
The BreakBeat Poets Vol. 3: Halal If You Hear Me
edited by Fatimah Asghar and Safia Elhillo
Commando by E'mon Lauren
Build Yourself a Boat by Camonghne Felix
Milwaukee Avenue by Kevin Coval
Bloodstone Cowboy by Kara Jackson
Everything Must Go by Kevin Coval, illustrated by Langston Allston
Can I Kick It? by Idris Goodwin
The BreakBeat Poets Vol. 4: LatiNEXT
edited by Felicia Rose Chavez, José Olivarez, and Willie Perdomo
Too Much Midnight by Krista Franklin
The Anti-Racist Writing Workshop by Felicia Rose Chavez
Dopplegangbanger by Cortney Lamar Charleston

Mama Phife Represents

Cheryl Boyce-Taylor

Haymarket Books
Chicago, Illinois

Published in 2021 by
Haymarket Books
P.O. Box 180165
Chicago, IL 60618
773-583-7884
www.haymarketbooks.org
info@haymarketbooks.org

ISBN: 978-1-64259-266-5

Distributed to the trade in the US through Consortium Book Sales and
Distribution (www.cbsd.com) and internationally through Ingram Publisher
Services International (www.ingramcontent.com).

This book was published with the generous support of Lannan Foundation
and Wallace Action Fund.

Special discounts are available for bulk purchases by organizations and
institutions. Please email orders@haymarketbooks.org for more information.

Cover artwork by Makeba Rainey, using the self-portrait photograph taken
by Malik Izaak Taylor, courtesty of Trini Gladiator LLC.

Printed in Canada by union labor.

Library of Congress Cataloging-in-Publication data is available.

10 9 8 7 6 5 4 3 2 1

For
Malik Izaak Boyce Taylor
and for
Phife Dawg
& Deisha Head Taylor

Didn't come 2 start trouble
Just 2 make the party bubble.
Earn a nice amount-a-green
build a mall in Southern Queenz.

—Phife Dawg

Look at spirit, how it fuses with earth giving it new life.

—Rumi

Contents

Interiors

Mama Phife Represents is a patchwork quilt that follows the journey of a mother's grieving heart. It is a hybrid book that recalls the death of a beloved son and follows his mother's first two years of public and private mourning. The story is told through a tapestry of narrative poems, dreams, anecdotes, journal entries, and letters. These treasured fragments of their lives together show the great love between mother and son, artist and artist, teacher and friend. This gift from Mama Phife, better known as Cheryl Boyce-Taylor, includes drawings, emails, hip-hop lyrics, and notes Malik Taylor, artistically known as Phife Dawg, wrote to his parents beginning at age eight. It concludes with lyrics from Phife Dawg's solo album, which he completed about two weeks before his death.

In the weeks and months following her son's death, Boyce-Taylor wrote to stay sane. She shares some of her happiest memories of Malik as a baby and young man. His strength and courage have been her guiding force. She returns to their early years to guide her through the most difficult time of her life. It was a way to help her believe that she could and would survive her nightmare.

Mama Phife Represents is not a linear text. It is blended to bring to the reader both elegy and praise song. Here there is joy, there is sorrow, there is healing, and a mother's triumphant heart rises and blooms again.

Introduction

I hid my pregnancy from my mother. But, sneaky detective that she was, she found out anyway. Mom had been snooping in my things when she found the "baby pills" (aka prenatal vitamins). She was the type of mother who knew better than you when to expect your monthlies. She knew if your period was late, if your heart was hurting, what boy was calling you on the downstairs telephone. I called her the pussy police. My mother knew all these intimate things about me, but was not able to speak to me about menstruation, sex, or birth control. So it's not surprising that I was not able to tell her that I was pregnant, despite the fact that I was engaged to my son's dad and that my family and I were making wedding plans.

Walt and I got married in July. Malik and his twin brother Mikal were born two months premature in November 1970, but only Malik survived. Walt and I are from Trinidad and became parents at nineteen and twenty-one; we had no clue about parenting. We were raised by the "children are seen and not heard" generation. Coming from Caribbean parents, we always joked that they were missing the nurturing gene; they were stern and had inherited an abundance of the punitive gene. So when our sons were born, we agreed to communicate openly with them and let them speak as much as they wanted to. In our home, Malik could discuss almost everything. He could not be rude or nasty, but he could share his thoughts and ideas freely. I had observed that many black men were not given the opportunity to express themselves freely in the US, and I did not want that for my child. We allowed him the freedom to think and dream . . . to fantasize and plan. I always taught my son to be a doer and not a talker. So when he announced that he was going to be a rapper, I could only support him.

1

As a young child, when looking at television together, our son would look at the toys on TV with stars in his eyes and say "I'm gettin' that!" Most children would probably say, "Mom, can you buy me that toy?" With him, it was, "I'm gettin' that!" He was a forceful child and knew at a very early age what he wanted for his future. Surprisingly, he had very good ideas and we never stopped his dreaming.

Once, when Malik was four, his grandmother left thirty-five cents for him to buy ice cream. When the ice cream truck rolled around, he was already in bed. Knowing how much he liked the music, I called him out of bed to see the truck. He wanted to go out and get some ice cream but it was already late and past his bedtime. When the truck left, he stomped into his room angry. I called out to him asking for my good night hug. He did not answer. I called him again. Still no answer. Finally, I said sternly, "Get in here. Did you hear Mommy saying good night to you?" He said "Yes, but I don't speak to people who don't stop ice cream trucks. My grandmother left money for my ice cream, and you let the truck go." I was stunned. There was no way to make it right, so I just hugged him and sent him to bed.

In nursery school Malik memorized every line of the play *Mother Goose*. He was able to prompt all the children who had forgotten their lines on the day of the show. In his third-grade yearbook he said he wanted to be an actor. It was in his blood, so we encouraged him to work hard and follow his art.

Phife, the artist, has so many fans around the world, but I share this story to give you a glimpse of Malik, the son, husband, diabetic, and dad. I share our story in hopes that it may inspire you to keep healing, growing, and moving forward even after you've been through the worst news of your life. It will take a lifetime for me to get over losing him, but I want you to learn from my story. When you've been given a life-threatening illness, you don't have to curl up and die. You can rise above the challenges and keep moving. As Tribe said, "push it along, push it along."

Additionally, I wrote this book for Deisha, Malik's wife, and David, his stepson. Mostly though, this is for Malik. For years I watched him struggle with the affliction of diabetes. There was a period when he would dialyze four times each day while on tour with A Tribe Called Quest. Sometimes he seemed too weak to perform, but he showed up. And when he hit that stage, he killed it! Watching his performnces remain some of my proudest moments as his mother.

I have learned courage, strength, determination, and love from Malik.   3
This is my story of faith and perseverance.

I. The Summer Phife Was Born

When Her Child Dies

for Malik

A mother does not know her heart
will leap out of her chest

with such force
it will cause a rebellion

she does not know
that her hands will be numb for weeks

she does not know her sugar will rise
even though she has not eaten in two days

she will come to distrust her universe

her black-eyed Susans her sweet Williams
the soil she loves to squish her toes in

sun hugging her aching shoulders
moon scurrying across her worn windowsill

she will mistrust them all

when her child dies
friends will come daily with milk honey

cheese red wine spelt bread & ginger jam
she will not remember their touch

only their eyes glossed over with tears
she does not know

8   she will stop speaking to his father
    and threaten to sue him

    her hair will fall out in clumps
    she will lose big spaces of memory

    when her child dies
    a woman will fight for her sanity

    she will travel to Anguilla
    beg Yemaya to bring him back

    as the ocean swells
    she will listen for his laughter

    she will press her face in the damp earth
    call his name

    Malik
    Malik
    Malik Izaak

Yellow Sour Grass

On the way to the burial
an embroidered lace of yellow oxalis
dotted the highway median

that mountain in me grew higher
littered with snapshots of his face
and the crude voice of earth's sorrow—

August 27, 1981

Dear Mom,

    Today I made up fifteen good songs.

Malik Taylor
(1981, age 10)

The Summer Phife Was Born

The year Malik was seven I was a theatre major at York College in Queens. When I could not afford a babysitter, I took him with me to class, poetry readings, and rehearsals. He would sit quietly and watch us rehearse, but mostly he would run around and play at the back of the theatre. It was there he met Imani, the little girl who was his best friend until the day he died. After playing for hours, I would ask him to settle down and write a poem, which he did cheerfully. His first poem was about being in the park after dark. A bit scary, but he had spent many hours at the park with his dad playing soccer, often into the late evening.

As a teenager he told me that he thoroughly enjoyed expressing himself on paper, and that it helped him to understand his questions more clearly. I felt overjoyed because I was raising a black man in troubled America who was seeking answers for some of his issues and questions.

The summer Malik was ten we were making plans to send him to YMCA summer camp in Jamaica, Queens, again when he told me how he hated that camp and did not want to go anymore. He had spent three previous summers there and seemed to really like it. I wanted to know why he didn't want to go anymore. He told me that the children fought and cussed a lot and that he'd rather stay home with his grandmother. She was a lot of fun and they did things together like visit family, shop for fruit, study his bible lessons, and cook. They even went to vacation bible school together. I knew lots of playtime was secretly woven into that righteous listing, so I made him a scrapbook and asked him to record his thoughts and send me a note every day telling me how he was and what he was doing. The first note went something like: "Malik played in the hot sun today, scrimmage and baseball, then he rested with a cool piece of watermelon. Grandma got stung by a bee and Malik did too." That was the beginning of a series of letters, journal entries, poems, and songs he wrote to his dad and me that year.

I will always believe Phife was born that summer.

7/24/81

Dear Malik,

You may not realize it now, and I know you think I am a mean, old, mother, but one day you'll realize that all my fussing, yelling and spankings were just as painful for me as it is for you.

I want you to be a success in everything you do thats why all the nagging.

So write me a letter each day telling me of your activities and how you're getting along. It will help you to express real feelings and make you a better writer.

Love Mom

7/24/81

Dear Malik,

You may not realize it now, and I know you think I am a mean, old, mother, but one day you'll realize that all my fussing, yelling and spankings were just as painful for me as it is for you.

I want you to be a success in everything you do that's why all the nagging.

So write me a letter each day telling me of your activities and how you're getting along. It will help you to express real feelings and make you a better writer.

Love Mom

Letters, poems, and lyrics arrived that summer, then "Rapper's Delight," RUN DMC, and LL Cool J swarmed our living room. Rap and hip-hop became staples of Malik's life. It was not long before he learned the pleasure of words spoken with music. Our home was a haven for political music and poems; we listened to Gil Scott Heron, Amiri Baraka, The Last Poets, Dick Gregory, Angela Davis, Nikki Giovanni, Sonia Sanchez, The Mighty Sparrow, Lord Kitchener, and most of all Bob Marley.

When Malik was eight my mother spent six weeks helping him memorize Dr. Martin Luther King Jr.'s "I Have a Dream" speech for a church cotillion. He did really well and received lots of encouragement and praise. A light switch went on; he carried it throughout his life.

A Piece of My Mind

Hey people I hate to say this but
younger brothers around here hanging out on the corners
and write graffiti on the mailbox.
They cut school and play Pac-Man (Galaxian), donkey Kong [sic] and they
never stop.
People (parents) you ought to give them a piece of your mind
because when they get old they show no they should have studied.
So people give them a piece of your mind.

Malik Taylor
    1980 (age 9)

St. Albans, NY

***

August 26, 1981

When I woke up this morning I was worried about my mom.
the phone rang and now I'll see who is home. So the person answered
and it was my father. So I woke up and bathe, ate breakfast.
I was reading the newspaper about a boy who was
killed by some Brooklyn bullies. He got shot through his thigh
and his back. Lascell Campbell murdered for his bike.
I thank God for not letting me die so young.

    Leke*
    1981 (Age 10)

*Leke is our family's nickname for Malik

I loved it in Baltimore, Maryland. It was very nice It was sunny & very Hot. They had these beautiful apartments. The second day we were there, we went out all day we went to Howard Johnsons For a beautiful breakfast then we headed for the Nations Capitol. Washington D.C. And we saw the White House. Then we were back and we went to the Harbor It was fun. And I saw people with Baltimore Orioles hats on and Colts. It was so beautiful I mean beautiful.

It was not dirty. It was very clean and very Quiet. While we were coming to Baltimore. We saw a place that looks like the country side. and they served snacks at a snack bar. When we reached Baltimore we went up the stairs and the place was very small compared to the station in New-York. Then suddenly Mike came and He got Lost but we found our way very safely.

Then we were in the house and we saw alot of space In the house and a terrace out side.

Then Mom and I looked at Television. And eating Potato chips and went to Sleep

*

This howl of ache
is ripping my throat
each time I raise my chin
a machete is thrown

there's blood on my knees
purple morning glories cover my window

downstairs Ana's salsa is loud
tribute to our lady of Guadalupe

I am crouched in a small space
trying to relearn my eyes

trying to remember
how joy lingers

18 Kiss

I want to kiss my child again and again
New Jersey ferry terminal where I last held his hand
memorized every holy road in the country of his beautiful face

*

My palm holds the map of your bodies   two tulip bulbs   in brown paper bag
hiding in the dark   under kitchen counter   waiting to flower

*

At nineteen his fish body sliced through
the warm embroidery of my bloodline
I held my baby   stout and cherished

the first one to touch his face
I was never alone
for years I wore a baby on my hip

held a baby to my lips
I was never alone

that child with a shimmering Afro
oh   the secrets birth thighs keep
and damn the lessons hearts yield

I can't hold you now

I am alone but not really alone love
in the quiet of this night
I'm missing you
the way a weight makes one
out of breath

Sometimes I feel like the child   left

Dear Mom,

Today Malik is eleven months old.

Yesterday he played baby Jesus in the manger.
This is his first play. He slept almost through the
entire thing. My friends, Lynrod and Leisa, are
Mary and Joseph.

Mom, there is an actual old shed with real straw
for the manger. I know we are growing something
special here. Walt and Cheryl are proud parents.

Cheryl.

Vida

Remember now
> *no carbs*
plantains
> *bread*
potatoes
bananas
no beer   grapes   corn   cheese   pasta   avocados

my doctor is so proud of the eighteen pounds I've lost

pain has slimmed me

weight loss, good for the pacemaker he says
I want to say, *fuck that pacemaker*
my heart, it's really fucking broken

they give me a huge blue gown
a bonnet to cover my curls
after three failed attempts at taking blood she gets it

they take all my possessions: my Tribe Called Quest socks,
my medical alert bracelet
and even my new panties with the cute little strawberry cupcakes
my wife takes my wedding rings
I sob and I sob

the OR is cold
a pretty Caribbean nurse from St. Lucia brings me two heated blankets
I tell her my mom was an OR nurse
sob even harder
she kisses me on the forehead

you need ripe plantains to keep your feet planted, Grandma used to say
who doz listen to American doctors?

not quite sure I trust this pacemaker
still making friends with it
I've named her Vida
after my mother's fiercest and meanest sister

Stitched

I've stitched your breath to my throat
child did your last howl resemble mine?

all day I want to sit in ashes
all the stars have followed you

since you've been gone

this left hand has betrayed me
has grown into my mother's

my index finger so crooked
it refuses to wash clean the dinner dishes

my eyes too are disobedient

I've told them not to tear
at the wound of the name son

does it listen?
did I say how lost I am?

your mom has a pacemaker Malik
that rebuilt heart too makes promises

it will rescue me   will sing pretty
will rebuild the heave and steam of my body

each night it takes a thigh a breast a begging skull
an arthritic knee

all around there are unhinged bones
wailing at the lip of sea

*

I miss my child's morning voice as I wake him on his birthday miss the way he says:

> *Ma tell me about my twin brother/and what time was I born Ma/and
> how many pounds did I weigh again/and when did you get to hold me
> Ma/how long did I live in my incubator/and tell me Mama the story
> about how I was born first/before my twin Mikal in the labor room/
> and how the doctors scurried around when they heard the loud hollering
> baby A/and how they came to find baby B on his way out/after you had
> told them repeatedly that you were a twin/and that you were having
> twins/how did you know this Mama/tell me Ma how you and Dad
> threatened the doctors/that you'd sign me out of Mary Immaculate hos-
> pital/that you'd take me home without consent/take me home because I
> was yours/because my crib was ready/with the white blankets/the white
> curtains/the blue heart-shaped pillows Grandma sewed/and the rocking
> chair Dad painted white/*

Tell me Ma . . .

120th Avenue, St. Albans, New York

Until now, I never told anyone
once, as a baby, Malik fell in a metal phone booth

from phone book rack
to metal floor, he fell

I grabbed him up
raced across 120th Avenue

without looking left or right
tears sliding down my face

once inside the door
I zipped him out of his thick baby-blue snowsuit

scared he was dead
examined him from nose to toes

still asleep, I held him tight
and swore never to tell a soul

not his father, grandmother, or uncle Russell
not Christine or my best friend Rose
no one . . . until now.

*

Standing with the first-grade boy
waiting to cross the light
he said, see you later, Ma,
I know my way to school
I want to walk alone

I walked two blocks behind
he bounced fearless through the tall green iron gates of PS 36

Pray

He stood near my bed one hand jammed in his pocket
his thinking cap on slightly crooked
he surveyed my face
then the delightful boy of seven said
Mommy do you pray?
Yes Malik
I responded
Mommy he said more sternly *what words do you say?*

All the parents come to church except you two
I don't want to go to heaven and my parents are lost
I am almost ready to be baptized you know
I looked at my little Christian boy
and did not have the heart to tell him
we don't go to church on Saturdays babe
we stay home to watch Soul Train

1970

My baby was born with a long wisp of hair stuck to his forehead. I had been in pain for two days before his birth. I went to the hospital, but they sent me back home. On the second day I returned, refused to leave. The next morning the doctors induced labor. I was seven months pregnant. I was parked on a bed in the labor area when I asked a nurse for a bed pan, she said, *No. You don't need one.* I got so angry. I said, *Okay! I'm going to shit up this bed!*

Moments after she left the room, I felt deep pressure and overwhelming pain . . . all I could do was push. And in what seemed like seconds, my boy was there—my gift—hollering to break free.

The doctors appeared like a swarm of bees all trying to make sure the baby was okay, but we had another surprise for them. Baby number two was on the way out. Mikal, Malik's twin brother. Since Malik's birth, I have often wondered how he picked my silly teen body to be his home. How and why did he choose me to be his mama?

Mikal only lived for eight hours, yet for years Malik spoke about him like he really knew him. As a young child Malik would tell his father and I that Mikal was coming to visit him. He often prayed for him before bedtime. Once he sang a song to us that he said his brother wrote. Later he wrote hip-hop lyrics for Mikal and acknowledged him on his ATCQ albums.

30

*

Orchids grew lush in that empty house
        ill-shaped with winter
        the year my twins were born
        the first came too soon
eyes brown tourmaline
        slick as rain puddles
he came a small wiry flame
mouth a red city
hands dark as the Volta River

the second barely cried
        no bells no wind
        no fire no flowers
I stood and fell
fell and stood torn away at the root
an exquisite ache at the grounding

Bati-Ethiopian Kitchen

Ceni my beloved calls the dark brown ground chicken
poop
she appeases me and has two glasses
of the wine that's too dry for her palate

a woman speaks loudly about the roommate who keeps wearing her clothes
and flirting with her man. We have just returned from picking up our save-
the-date invitations for our ceremony. The printing place messed up and gave
us the wrong size. They fix it by giving us a 50 percent discount and eighty
postage stamps. We are thrilled. We have the world by its chin. We order
champagne and make a toast to our future. We have been together twenty
years. We are sweetly in love.

    We make a second toast to our wedding
    she calls it our "party"
    I say "wedding"

How lovely it sounds rolling off my tongue.

Malik loved his wife and her son David
They loved him back

She gave him a kidney instead of a baby
We rejoiced at that new birth
a kidney baby

Outside on Fulton Street we hear tree chimes
we hear fire engines and happy people clapping inside Greenlight Books.
    It's the beginning of spring.

We arrive home tipsy   fall into each other's arms
Ceni hands me the phone

32   eight missed calls from Deisha and Roots
     My heart speeds up   damn

               I lay on the bed scared to touch the phone It rings
               rings again
                              fear
               fear grows

     Cheryl are you up? It's Deish.
     Wake up. I need to talk to you.

     Cheryl . . . Cheryl—

     *

               All the phones are ringing
               even our land line

               Mom, Cheryl, it's Jarobi.
               The press is hounding us, what do you want to say?

               Ceni looks at me, the rich tapestry of her face cracking
               the wreckage of my body strewn across the room

               Mom, I can't reach Walt. Have you spoken to him yet?

               Robi, I can't talk now.

               Mom, TMZ has called again. What do you want to say?

     Say something sweet about my child.

     My son has died in California and I fear getting on the plane.

*

When Malik was six or seven, Walt and I were looking at our wedding pictures with him. Suddenly he began to cry. We asked him why and he said, "You didn't let me come to the wedding. I wasn't at the wedding" And he was just sobbing. We hugged him. Then I told him, "Oh yes you were. You were in Mommy's tummy." It soothed him for a moment. But later that summer he came to me and said, "You and Dad got married in July." I answered, "Yes." "And I was born in November?" There was mischief on his face as he rapidly counted the numbers on his fingers. Then he gave me that disapproving look of his and said, "Oh Mom . . . ohhhh Mommmmm," and walked away stunned. Our child had a moral compass. That was the first of many questions he would ask about our intimate life. I answered each question as honestly as I could, not forgetting that I had been raised with a Caribbean strict gene. And with each answer, he would have his own personal comments . . . and often judgments . . . or hysterical laughter. But his dad and I were committed to being open and loving parents . . . less critical and with fewer secrets than when we were brought up.

People's Instinctive Travels

and the Paths of Rhythm

It was the end of his eighth grade. That fall our son would be going to boarding school. It was the most painful year for the three of us. After almost eighteen years of marriage his father and I were divorcing. Our son was hurting and so was my mother, who had been a second mom to him. Her only grandchild, the apple of her eye, as she put it, was leaving home. That Christmas he let me know, in his very angry voice, that he was *never* getting married. He said that he hated the way we had conducted the last few years of our marriage.

What does a parent say?

Malik was particularly displeased with me because he believed, like his dad, that I had ruined our marriage and our home life. It would be years before I would get out from under all that guilt. It broke my heart that we had hurt him so much. I resolved to make it up to him. And I did. Yes, God, I did!

The next few years for him were very tough. He seemed aimless and lost, then he found hip-hop. So when, on that sunny October day, he told me he was leaving high school to go on tour with A Tribe Called Quest, I was over-joyed, but scared and sad at the same time. I was thrilled that he had found his sweet spot. Joy and excitement had returned to his spirit. I didn't dare say no. I watched my teenage son pack his bags and head to Europe. His very own *People's Instinctive Travels and the Paths of Rhythm*.

*

*Mom I'm moving to Atlanta/I'm sick of being the only child/
only grandchild/only nephew/
y'all smother me to death/I got to live/*

*

Mom, I'm going on tour with A Tribe Called Quest, we are going to Europe.

*

*(Malik calling from London)
Family, I'm headed home tomorrow. I'm off this
tour, these folks won't give me a chance to showcase. They want me to do back up
for Q-Tip, this ain't no Diana Ross and the Supremes thing
I ain't backing up nobody . . .
I'm here to kick my rhymes and show my skills.*

*

*And Mom, I met a girl, Deisha, she reminds me of you. She has African paintings
in her house just like you, Mom, she has natural hair, "no long extensions," no,
natural hair.
She loves sports and hip-hop and she's hella sweet.
I think she's the one.*

*

*Family, D. is my match.
She's from California, has a two-year-old son, his name is David.
Wow, I love that kid, he is funny and great to be around.
This is feeling good.
—Malik*

Deisha Comes Home

Malik brings Deisha home to meet Grandma
Grandma is the apple of his eye
he wants her approval first

When I meet her they are talking
basketball and football
She's a Raiders fan

She's West Coast sweet
loves East Coast hip-hop

I pay attention to the way they hold hands
She brings him tea with one Equal one Splenda

At Thanksgiving that year
our whole family gathers at Malik's house
We are a loud and rowdy bunch
We meet Deisha's son David for the first time
He's two years old and frightened by the noise
hides his face in Malik's chest
He holds him close

We see for the first time he's a dad
We fall in love with that little boy

early one Sunday morning my son calls
he's pumped and filled with music
tell me about you and Dad, about my birth, Mom
he wants every detail, he's working on a new project
a new song for Deisha

I tell everything I can remember
I know he's gathering feed for lyrics

I want to know about my first night home/
Dad said/ I cried and cried all night/
that you took turns walking me up and down the halls/
and did you say, Mom, that you and Dad
put tiny band-aids at the edge of my pacifier
to hold it in my mouth?/you
my silly teen parents in your youthful ignorance

I like the part, Ma/
when you called the hospital at 3 a.m./
to find my doctor to tell him about my nonstop cries/
tell me how he said/

put a tiny radio in the baby's crib/
with the music on low/after three months in the hospital/
he's used to lights and noise all night/

is that what the doctor said?/tell me again, Mom/
Dad, I want to know/
is that when my love of music started?/
is that why for all of my adult life I've stayed up late?/
just my music and me/

tell me again, Mom/ how you believed that night/that very night
I fell in love with music/me and my little transistor radio/
that night I fell in love with music/
and never/ never gave her up/

In Malik's Bathroom Drawer

Fantasia's CD *Back to Me*
Lloyd Banks's CD *The Hunger for More*
backstage passes for Super Bowl XlVII
New Orleans, Gate E
row 7, seat 21
price $950.00
The Isley Brothers *Live!*
two wide-lined notebooks
one white one yellow
a One Touch Ultra Soft Lancet
ATCQ *The Low End Theory* cassette tape
a copy of *Raw Air* by CBT
an unknown number of pennies
Webster's New World Dictionary
Novolin and 70/30 insulin
Bob Marley & the Wailers CD *Gold*
Phife Dawg's *Ventilation da LP*
De La's CD *3 Feet High and Rising*
wedding picture of Malik and Grandma Elma

*

In April 1998, ATCQ released their first album: People's Instinctive Travels and the Paths of Rhythms.
What a genius title.

*

By spring 1991, Tribe released a new album called: The Low End Theory. *It was that year that Malik first complained of blurred vision and fatigue. We were certain it was from his work, but after seeing a doctor we got the bad news that, like me, he was suffering from Type 1 Diabetes.*
I was totally heartbroken and wondered if he should quit the group, however he was treated and continued working and touring.

*

Family, I am working hard and loving this music, but I'm really struggling with my health; the doctor says sooner or later I may need a kidney transplant.

*

Tour is going well and we are working on a new album. Things are just great with Deisha and I . . . I think I'm going to marry that girl. And if we have a baby we are not calling him Boyce . . .
I know you love that name mama, but I prefer Marley.
And get this . . . David loves the name Boyce; he says he'll take it.
Funny kid.

(On a visit home to New York.)
*

Mom, I'm getting worried about the kidney search.
What if I don't make it?
Mom, can I lie down with you?

*

Mom, Deisha and I getting married—will you walk me down the aisle?

I visited the kidney clinic again today and my doctor says I need dialysis. I am choosing peritoneal dialysis for two reasons

1. I can administer it myself.

2. It's the only way I can keep traveling with my group. I'm not giving that up. I will have to dialyze four times a day, but so be it that's the choice. This is hard and I'm not happy, but I'm pushing ahead.
Love,
—M.

Our last summer together

I introduce Malik to Andra Day
we listen together
quiet/intense   he puts "Rise UP" on repeat
it is our favorite song
a huge smile creases his face/he hugs me hard/no words

for my birthday in December he gives me *Cheers to the Fall*
I sit it on my dresser in its tight plastic wrap
I have not opened it yet

my sweet boy skin of smooth bamboo
I promised the wind never to forget your arms
to carry an ocean in my heart
to spend a whole life watching it grow
I am thinking of my baby boy's chest
Prussian blue
how it rose
and fell
rolling faint
faint against my fingertips

Dear Mom,

I am angry
deprived
my child
my child
my friend
anchor
companion
my grace
my laugh magnet
my first born

                              Gone—

Cheryl,

*

Last night a rainstorm called me bitter
I said, "No!"
beautiful mother
beautiful mother

Fuck and Fuck

how many little things can I kill? how many
before I get revenge?   how many killings
before satisfaction? roaches honeybees flies mosquitoes crickets June bugs
how many little things can I kill before I get even with nature? red ants black
ants fruit flies
kitchen flies spiders snakes
how many small things can I kill before I am whole again?

Notes for My Son's Care

Journal entries

Things to go over with Malik and Deisha
Personal things Malik needs for his care (once he is home from the hospital)

1. meds and supplies in 2nd-floor bedroom
2. recliner to do meds
3. chair for the porch
4. shower curtain in 2nd-floor bathroom
5. shades in master bathroom
6. ~~shades in master bedroom~~
7. visiting nurse
8. transportation to HEMO
9. someone to prepare 2 meals per day
10. home delivery food service
11. pure organic foods
12. chair for the living room
13. housekeeping service

FINANCES:
What is Malik's bank account balance?
Monthly medical expenses/outstanding bills
Does he owe IRS any money?
Ticket for grandma to visit
Last-minute ticket for Dad to get here

The Morning after Transplant Surgery (October 9, 2008)

My friend Donna Lee walks Malik
around the hospital ward
he is shaky on this first walk
he heads to his wife's room
I'm scared for her
her entire family is at the hospital
dear God   I pray and pray

instead of a baby she has given him her kidney

they hug careful not to bruise anything
we look away
out the window into a glorious blue San Francisco day
gray and white mountains

Bob Marley

As his parents argued loudly in the living room, the clever boy of six sat on the living room sofa and began to sing softly:

> *If you get down and you quarrel every day you are going to live in the negative, negative way.*

—Bob Marley

We fell over laughing and the fight was over.
Bob Marley was our family guru then.

II. Apricot Begonias

Apricot Begonias

The week of the burial

1.

Two months after my son's death my friend Sabrina buys us tickets for
Mexico City   she says we are going on a pilgrimage to visit Frida Kahlo
She is fluent in Spanish   says she will take care of me   every evening
she makes ginger tea and hugs me tight

She finds us an Airbnb in a small scenic art district   three times
we get locked out before we learn the key combinations   in the middle
of the living room there's a hammock with a view of the bridge   ahead
of the fog we see Mexico City rising in the distance   I've come late to this
grief

We visit Frida in Coyoacán   At Lomas Verdes in an open square filled
with children and women wearing colorful off-the-shoulder dresses we listen to
folk music   and men dressed in charro suits singing *Besame Mucho* We eat
tostadas frijoles authentic mole chicken flautas with ceviche and guacamole

Watch the body bend and curve   watch it shudder watch the body
an endless aching fire giving twin souls back to soil   I have not spoken in
days

The begonia leaves have grown small white dots   *sorry for your loss honey*
did you remember to blow out the white candles?   honey did you dust the
Tribe Called Quest CDs?   the guests will want to see them   have we called
the funeral director maybe we should sage the house
        I forgot   did you find a frame for it   the poem I mean the poem

2.

Apricot begonias are my favorite flowers   will you hold my hand love?

we marry in the middle of all that sorrow   after twenty years she is my wife
did we order begonias

                        are spider mums in bloom?
        baby shall we order fresh Long Island peaches for the repass?

50   WIFE   wife   my wife   the wedding cake has two tiers   we dance to Beyonce's *Love on Top*   the guests join in we walk each other down the aisle   we have never been happier   wife   wife   I follow her around and scratch for something to pray to   I follow her like a flock of wild turkeys   all my cells looking for something to hold to cling to belong to

baby turkeys are called poults   my baby is called too soon

female turkeys are called hens will you hold my heart up to the light beards on male turkeys are called gobblers   grief on a bride   is called

Will you make me a cup of rooibos tea with acai berry   cup   of   wild sweet

orange   are we expecting companyshould I fold the throw rugs? fluff the sofa pillows?   will we serve South African Malbec?

sorry for your loss   *your*   *for loss*

The poets come to our home   with sage white candles and Florida water
they bring white calla lilies my son's favorite flower   they bring drums koras
and shekeres   they make a joyful noise form a prayer circle   Elana
leads all in song   we hug each other   a laying on of hands
we howl and pray together   I feel lifted

        Harmattan something close to lightning and sand-
    storm

did we remember to turn off the bathroom light?   In Trinidad we put the
top tier of the wedding cake in the freezer   save it for one year   have
you had anything to eat?

    Will you bring my writing pen and paper?   will the robins return
for grain?   is the door locked will everyone leave before sunrise?
what day is it?   has the cat been fed?   use the good dishes in the glass
cabinet love   will I see my son again?   can I?   On his first walk after
transplant surgery Malik walks to his wife's room   she has given him her
kidney   we love our kidney baby   we love Deisha

    Malik sends me purple irises for my birthday   *Mom I found my girl she
reminds me of you* What time will the funeral cars be here   will you put on
the kettle?   will we begin with the flutes of Carlos Nakai or Bob Marley?

4.

Will you pray with me?   I go to Yemaya
Jesse and Eric meet me in Anguilla
we listen   waves lick the sand like an obedient lover   we have fried conch and
lukewarm eggnog   at dinner the mixed drinks are weak   flies
never leave the table   The black and white couple next door talks too
much   all night incessant talking and bragging   we laugh in odd places
don't hear a word they're saying   there's dried toast no milk for cappuccino
we discuss the poems of Aracelis Girmay read letters from Frida to Diego
love the dialect of Michelle Cliff in *Land of Look Behind*   in the morning
we search the island for fried bake and bacalao   we look for a wicker

52   frame for my new poem   night rolls in heavy as sorrow   my twin sons
Malik and Mikal are the butter yellow butterflies who greet me every morning
they walk me to the breakfast shed

   Mom I need a kidney   will you lay with me?

   dear mountain my heart is still not healing

   I fill the bathroom with begonias and baby's breath   my bath water
is so hot it makes me weep

   where has my son gone   why did he leave I love it when he calls
me Mama Phife calls me gal and boo   calls me Mama and Mami o n c e
when he was twenty I told him he could call me Cheryl   he said hell no
imma call you Mama   and Sista

                        Watch the body bend and curve   watch it
                        shudder watch the
body this gift an endless aching fire giving twin souls back to the land

Mom Deisha and I have a son his name is David   Mom I am so in love
with that little guy

    Mom can I get in bed with you   M o m
I   don't   think   I'm   gonna   make   it
    I held that knife inside thought it would kill me

    Mom thank you for your unconditional love and guidance
    you have always stood by me Mama Sista
    I love you like no other—

sorry for your for your   lossssorry
your loss   tonight I want to hold the rain

my mother bury she husband who fall from heart attack in de morning
    and my mother bury she second chile, a son, who fall from heart attack dat
evening my mother bury both ah dem next day and not one time not one time she
even ask the earth why
    sorry for your loss   Fitzroy the cab driver who took me to the ferry in
Anguilla   With these tears I have made war
sorrow a blue Angel crashing against my teeth   grief is a dangerous
widow forgetting names of   To walk alone   t h e
deep side of river I think it's Monday   are the neighbors here?   *s o r r y*
    I have come to love Maker's Mark   honey when will the sun return?
three shots of whiskey   Cheryl Allison, age thirteen, leaving
Trinidad
    1964 arriving alone to New York City my parents no longer speak to
each other   Dad takes me to the airport   holds my hand
Mom lost somewhere in that hospital bed *sorry*   praise the daughter in
me and the brave son who carries my poetry   praise   him

6.

Cerulean color of Swazi Gods
After our son's death
we poured colored sugar over our cereal to keep our love sweet

7.

My daughter-in-law and I bring our arms full of grief to Annie's massage table
it is in a sweet cottage on the grounds of the lavish Coronado Hotel on the
West Coast
where Marilyn Monroe filmed *Some Like It Hot* in 1958
    You lay on Annie's table soft eucalyptus and bergamot oils fill the room
    Annie says let me shift your sorrow and mama just cry cry mama
    outside pregnant women walk the beach with mothers sisters lovers
    a chicken coop brood of children

    you watch a one-year-old boy take his first steps he tumbles over with
each half step he gets up grins tumbles again his screeches fill the impossible
length of ocean
    Once at the beach in Tobago we made paper boats sailed them
    to God knows where
    damn Malik   I thought I'd have you forever
    to be that small boy walking for the first time   red shirt blue overalls
    bald head   three shiny new teeth

    could not go to the site to bury the body
    hold me
    I fear I'll never speak again
    finally my lips apart   hissing

Stone

That first night after you left
I saw God's face
and wept bitterly

The second night God offered
a prayer
I screamed that prayer away

The third night God reached
out his hand
I chewed on it until it became dust

On the fourth night
my tears became stone
that filled in for eyes

Six months later when they broke
my heart open there was not much
just cloves and blue leaves

Gift: One Sweet Braid Down She Back

We gave the earth his voice, his bones.
And he is not fading. And he is not not gone.

—William Fogarty

I want thirty more years of poems
I want tiger lily poems
orange blossom poems   mango poems
and poems by Lucille Clifton and   Suheir Hammad
        poems by Dionne Brand and Joy Harjo
I want Grace Jones to sing she "Bumper song," sweet and lawless
doh care a damn what nobody feel
I want Jamaican yard talk poems   how I love that Nannie ah de Maroons
talk
        gimme some Trini bush poems
spiked with Vat 19 Rum
and plenty blue hundred-dollar bills
lots and lots and lots of blue bills so Mami cud just stay home and brush she
hair and count bills
        and make flying fish and dumplings and count blue bills and
make new babies with names like
tamarind and flambeau

        names like righteous and kneel-n-pray
names like one sweet braid down she back
        names like earth morning star and inhabited

        poems to light white candles for good luck spells poems that blow
kerosene and inspire rage poems to taunt the gods and almost get them vex
let Mami cut oil drums to make steel pan
and rock melodies until my dead
twin brother come walking unshaven in de yard
with Malik on he arm   an say
all right all'yuh I home again

ah done roaming

ah home safe
ah home
now what all'yuh want meh do

we light ah big yard fire make pigtail soup and homemade Guinness stout ice cream this time around de girls go churn de ice de boys go pour de salt we go praise sing for we dead

  we go drink old oak rum rub a little on de chiren gums
  we go brew mauby bark and sorrel
  an at sixty-seven granny go collect fresh blood an child-bear again
  Cheryl an Mami go get back de twins dey lost

III. Mama Phife

Mama Phife

He calls me Mama PHIFE
All his friends call me Mama Phife
I love how that sounds
I love how he says
what's up Ma

I say nothing   what about you

I love how he always says Cool cool
and when he hangs up he says   *Luv ya Ma*

then he says: *ONE* (One Love)
I'm never sure which one it is
the number "1"
or the word "one"

        My son always called my mother and me Ma
and when he said Ma, we were never sure which one he was
calling

Dear sunrise I break with each dawn waiting for his voice

Dear Malik,

forgive the years when as a teen
I became your mother
forgive me
when I disrespected you
forgive me
when I failed to listen
forgive the years
when you felt like an unloved teen
dull without your mother's shine
forgive the wound that broke you from throat
to fractured toe
forgive me

Love,
Mom

1.
For the record
I just want you to know, Mom
you are everything to me,
I'm elated to have you as my, Mom
and as I get older
I feel more and more like a momma's boy

2.
Mom
only a few people affect me in a positive way
(by what they do, say, and how they live)
w/out being hypocritical
although I didn't always do right in my younger years, and made it almost
impossible to cope
with me I thank you from the bottom of my heart
For sticking with my hardheaded ASS, supporting my career,
I thank you for loving my wife and child and giving me (sometimes) crazy/
insane advice!
I love you unconditionally, I'm excited that you're coming 2 Denver!
You may as well come with me 2 Seattle
LOL! Love

PS let's cancel these assholes in our lives.
(Leke)

Malik Calling from J Dilla's House

Phone would ring
pring pring
"Ma   Sistre   yuh good   whad up
hear what
I working on a benefit here with JD's mom
when I done I'mma swing thru New York and pick yuh up
we go head Toronto for a Raptors game
just a bit of mama and son chat up
pack lite
love yuh Sistren
love yuh Boo
one"

I'd grin wide and know he was up in he Trini ting dat day
I'd pull a bag and start to pack
in awe of that man.

Tribe Called Quest Disbands!

I will never forget the day that I saw that headline plastered about the big news stand in Union Square. At the time I worked as a case manager in New York City. Malik and I had been discussing some of the issues the group was having the past year. To me, the discussions seemed to be in progress ... more conversation than certainty. So when I left my job and headed home after work that day, I was stunned to see the announcement. I was sad. As I rounded the corner headed into the subway, the big headline read: "Tribe Called Quest Disbands." My heart sank. This had been a big part of my child's adult life, the work he loved, the only work he ever knew. What would happen? Where would he go? I was confused.

There is no doubt that A Tribe Called Quest is and has been one of the most positive, influential game changers in the music industry. I am eternally proud of their contribution to hip-hop.

Without a doubt, there were very good years, years that netted them six great albums. But after years of touring and not getting along because of professional and personal conflicts, Tribe agreed to end it. As my son put it: "It's like dating your elementary school sweetheart when you're in college." For Malik, the decision to end it all was painful but freeing. For our family, it was a difficult time. Our son had worked very hard for his career. Starting over was not an option. Phife and Q-Tip were no longer close. Beef among brothers, egged on by industry folks, had come between them. While they deeply cared for each other and their families, the authentic respect of friendship and brotherhood was gone. The joy of making music was no longer present and they agreed to separate while still on top.

In the years that followed, they would travel and perform occasionally, but a sour note remained. The group began with three MCs and a DJ, but over the years Q-Tip became this self-imposed headman. And Phife was no follower. Like all good gladiators, he was headstrong, talented, and determined to move ahead. He rebuilt his work platform through sports commentating, music, and a solid, loving family life.

I am so proud of the work he did on the final album *We got it from Here ... Thank You 4 Your Service*. This work is centered around love, brotherhood, and deep political conviction. Phife's contribution was, as always, strong, hardcore, and amazing. I am grateful for my child and the lessons he left through his music, sports, and the life he lived.

66 Mama Phife Represents: Battle Rap

Phife keep he fiyah till de very end
never mind soothsayers and dumb niggas
        sugar could na break he
you think you
de Trinis say *is de answer dat doz bring de row*
snake dress up like sheep
but God don never sleep
meh boy was pure thunder an hurricane too
Mr. Phife was a boss man an ai say ai say dat

      so who want it wid de gladiator mama
she nah good food fer eat
crush yuh like mince meat
watch a scorpion fly
shady one tek we fer fool
bumba tek ah rest
Phife Dawg keep he fiyah til de dutty end

     now step off de damn bus friend   cha
tek yuh prozac

Valentine's Day 2009

Chicago

Malik and I are arguing on the phone
I said his little brother was a brat
I said he was a brat too
he listened
I was too angry to stop myself

that fight was our biggest blowup
over a planned family vacation
we hung up abruptly
next day he sent me a letter laced with childhood rage

Mom you are selfish
everything is about you
you show off Mom
with your education and your poetry
it's all about you always putting 50 on it

we didn't speak for two months

I never regretted that fight
that letter cut deeply
we never fought so passionately
never made up so lovingly

sometimes a parent has to eat their child's rage

weeks after your death
I could not look at the news
could not bear to see

Phife Dawg of
A Tribe Called Quest
1970–2016
RIP

it was all over the news   internet
radio   television   on the weather and sports stations
it was difficult to breathe to talk
I've grown to hate the letters "RIP"

in 1927 my grandma lost twin boys
I never figured out how she learned to sing after that

the ache of public mourning
good God the love that poured in sweet bitter   honey

When a House Lives Alone

for Walt & Malik

when a house lives alone
it is still filled with love
what remains goes unsettled in us

we pack up your bathroom
dad and I
I know you are laughing at us

this is what it has come to
mom and dad perfect strangers
packing up your house

there are bath towels
still tied with ribbons and store labels
two tubes of Tom's of Maine toothpaste
fennel and baking soda   dried in the tube

when a house lives alone
beds go unmade for weeks   months even
rubber soles of expensive sneakers melt together
we throw them out

in that long weekend of solitary packing
dinner looks like five-minute couscous and salad
oatmeal and raisins
a lone glass of shiraz

the father puts more wood on the fireplace
turns pages in an old album
you in daycare   you at eighth-grade graduation
you with your first gold album
on your feet crisp Air Force 1s

the mother makes peppermint tea
an altar of white sage and crystals
celebrate the fourth-year anniversary of her son's death

four years later tears still flow
this morning the same haunting questions
Malik were you happy?
did you know how much we loved you?

we pause at the mantle
a picture of us three in a green wood frame
mother father son
time is so unkind

did he call my name in that hour?
what did he know for sure?
was he still dreaming about having a child?

did the new album fill that space?
did he love me more than dad?
all I ever wanted was to be a good mother

that last night did he dream about his grandma?
was she at the gate to meet you?
by now you must be out of pain

I blow a kiss to no one in particular
to weep until exhaustion
to fold with pain

to weep with joy that too is the question
to weep with joy that too is the answer

On Brooklyn Nights

Moon over Eastern Parkway
What his hands left:
a new Tribe album
a solo CD
lawyers estates
rights of publicity
coming year projections
commercial use of name and likeness

My love and I marry in the middle of all that ache
six months after your death
we walked into our reception house C & C
on top the wedding cake "C & M"
proof you are still here and playing tricks on us

Fall 2018
a Phife sculpture is erected at Socrates Sculpture Garden in Astoria, NY
Queens City Council has renamed 192nd street in St. Albans
Malik "Phife Dawg" Taylor Way
when Deisha and I hoisted the sign

a bright orange light struck the world

To Dad, from Malik

Summer 1981
Trinidad

Otherwise things are okay I am
playing alot of small Goal.
I was in one fight with,
Desmond I won *of course.*

If you see John tell him
I said hi.

One of your tapes are
messed up, the song Sunshine
on Side B is tangled with
bad boy on Side A.

I want to come home with
Mom cause I hate Trinidad
because of mrs Taylor.

Love ya,
Malik

P.S, please buy me a pair of
Play boys for school (black) the ones
like yours. bye, bye.

To Dad, from Malik

Otherwise things are okay I am
playing a lot of small goal
I was in one fight with
Desmond
I won <u>of course</u>.

If you see John tell him
I said hi.

One of your tapes are
messed up, the song Sunshine
on side B is tangled with
bad boy on side A.

I want to come home with
Mom because I hate Trinidad
because of Mrs. Taylor.

Love you

Malik

P.S. please buy me a pair of
play boys for school (black) the ones
like yours. bye, bye.

Ships

In school boys and girls get award
for their achievment in the work they do
Their is a shipcalled scholar ship
For being smart in every subj F.
There another shipcalled citzen ship
For Attendance being on time never at +
hardly late, but the best ship i friends
having friends who cheer you up
when you deon and out.
Thats what friend are for.
When you are old and you still
have that same freind
he will help you & you will help him
anyway are friends for.

Malik
Taylor,

Ships

In school boys and girls get awards for their achievement in the work they do. [Is a ship called scholarship. For being smart in every subject. There is another ship called citizenship. For attendance being on time never absent hardly late, but the best ship is friendship having friends who cheer you up when you are down and out. That's what mine are for. When you are old and you still have that same freind he will hep you & you will help him anyway are friends for.

Malik Taylor

Crossing River

Dear Dad,
so many nights of incoherent mutterings
you cross river to soft marsh and dragonfly streams
Father be my guide on this blind walk through mourning

Dear Grandma Ada,
for twenty-four thousand four hundred and fifty-five mornings
I have carried your raging tongue
boiled cassava with fish and onion stew
on rainy Fridays like you taught me

stupes (suck teeth)
stupes when de hot pot burn meh hand

picked mint and sorrel leaves
from right outside yuh bedroom window Grandma
to wrap meh head in white cloth bed a makeshift tomb·
bright with bitter marigolds

grandmother did you find my Malik
new to that scrabble of land

Dear son, .
hold my hand
learn me your dance of surrender

Sweets, I thought I'd grow old with my palm in yours

                              Mom

Wesley Lake

I dream we are at the slave house in Goree
our spines fade   into the walls   a symphony of empty pots bang around
in the cool air
how sharply loss wounds the body
Sitting at the edge of Wesley Lake I ask my friend Jessica am   I   really
growing out of grief   Is my heart mending or am I kidding myself
Jessica who has eaten grief and lived to tell   so   I
a s k

That boy entered my house by the back door. Swallowed my joy then
made a poem. That year the boy learned to make spells Rap music to keep his
blues at bay. That man who prayed before each meal. That man who lived and
lived brave
That man who loved Knicks and Tar Heels Chaka Khan J Dilla and Stevie
Wonder

Imagine summer without Japanese azaleas their light paper wings   my
tongue heavy as a car tire   no son's shoulder to caress   no face to cup in palms
to braid my child's hair again   to make him beef stew   hear the pots sing   hear
him make jokes about my burnt curry   hear him laugh hard   watch his hands
in action when he makes his Sunday turkey burgers   on his face his daddy's
pride

Outside death's teeth stunned us into a kind of freeze   we walked
around zombie-like   mornings we woke   put the coffee pot on
flipped up the news the world
went   round
and round as usual
imagine that—

*

Our brilliant boy of four hosting his first birthday party,
Mom and Dad, he said, I want to host my own birthday party

Later he told his friends:
ladies and gentlemen, fasten your seat belts
And later:
Are you having fun, so how yuh likin' de party?

The summer before your death
I ate mostly cherries and watermelon in honor of the fruits you and Grandma
loved
Half-heartedly worked on the new book   drove you crazy with calls about what to
title it   we make suggestions find reasons to throw them out
How about—
In This New Light
I change the name three times before sending it to press
We settle on Arrival, in honor of the places we have arrived in life

Seven months later I am a mother without her child
What is the term for that?

April 4, 2016

*

Your father takes a picture . . .
poses himself in front of the open casket I want to crack that
motha-fucker's skull.
How dare he take a picture of our child in his casket! What good father
does that?
What good father does that?

Fuck why
were we tourists of your forgotten city
a lit cigarette hung low on the lip
bourbon your beautiful dark queen
that girl ran her fingers through your bleak summers
adoration passed heavy as blood

*

Cry cry scream cry scream break the planet body body break the planet/
even now I take a last slow look push my stomach into the blue metal box one
last time push and push so you touch your first home

*

How I adored that man who became my friend preacher teacher advisor
companion
that man taking interviews as he lay sick in his hospital bed
that boy who memorized Martin Luther King Jr.'s "I Have a Dream"
speech at six years old . . .
that boy who said prayers before each meal
that boy who bought his mother a house
that boy who knew how to cook
that boy whose body failed him time and time again that boy who knew to
rise/laugh/sing/love/his/Deish/his Kira & Kaylia/that/man/who loved his
son/Isley/Brothers/Charlie Wilson/Chaka Khan/James Brown/Grandma
Elma/loved his mama/father/Dr. Pepper/ATCQ/red solo/chicken roti/his
twin brother/

his/pockets/stuffed/gospel/blues/calypso/reggae/deep/ 79
    chutney bangra/jazz keys trailing from The Low End Theory/
marauding/at midnight/at midnight/

April 5, 2016

I thrash around in bed
scream at the window
rage in the shower

I wonder if God hears

I look to Privit
her lean brown frame
she gives me no answer just stands there
winking in her forest green eye shadow
wordless the mask of her stillness
visible on her tapered neck

I eat and eat from the table of loss

finally when it's all gone I want more
afraid to live with/without it I
miss the daily discipline of tears as company

miss the scorch
loss brings to my face
and please the morning stab of grief

Memphis, Tennessee, April 4, 1968
the day Martin Luther King Jr. was killed
        New York City, April 4, 2016
I buried my child
        I didn't notice until two weeks later
        how could that be

Hand of the Midwife

after Grandma Ada

My grandmother was a village midwife
not certified she delivered babies
shaped heads   broke fevers   flowed milk
buried umbilical cords and blue babies
a mix of blue cohosh   raspberry leaves
Clary sage skullcap root
Viburnum opulus   goldenseal
my grandmother's right hand was a sure shot it patched broken hearts
dried turmeric leaves to improve digestion
boiled tamarind leaves to treat jaundice and diabetes
it scrubbed and ironed until
it was stiff and sore   Grandmother

what medicine plant can I boil for this wounding

Blueberry Yogurt

Malik was shopping in the supermarket near his home when a white man cut the line and jumped in front of him. At first he was frustrated, but waved him on to go ahead. The man seemed irritated and started an argument with him. He called him stupid. Malik ignored the man, but the guy continued his tirade about nigger privilege and nigger out of their place. As he was walking away, Malik reached in his cart and took out a yogurt and threw it at the man. It hit him in the neck . . . a blueberry yogurt missile. The man held his neck and began to howl. In a second flat, Malik was out of there, in his car, and on his way home. Upset and frustrated, he called me. I tried to keep my voice casual as he told me. Then I broke out in uncontrollable laughter. Before long he was laughing too at the sheer absurdity of this encounter . . . blueberry yogurt!

Still the Sweetest Words I Ever Heard

My beloved grows right out of my own heart how much more union can there be.

—**Rumi**

Happy Mother's Day, Mom
I made this picture for you, Mom
Mom, Grandma is my bestest friend ever
Mom, I'm coming home for your birthday
Mom, the album went gold
Be my date for the Grammys

Mom, I found my girl, she reminds me of you Her name is Deisha
Mom, I have a son   His name is David
Mom, I love that little guy
Happy Birthday, Mommy

Mom, thank you so much for my laptop!!!
It is the best birthday present you ever gave me
I have been at home all weekend writing and making music
I swear, I'll never leave the house again
Words light life's path   Big ups Sista!

Mom, I'm so happy
I'm getting married
Will you walk me down the aisle?
Mom, I love you go on tour with me
Mom, you and Ceni move to California with me
You're getting kinda old
I mean good old!

San Diego, 2015

For three months, Malik was telling me he had a special surprise for my birthday. I tried to squeeze it out of him, and each week his texts got more elaborate. I tried to get Deisha to tell me. She would laugh and say that she didn't know what it was. Finally, December rolled around. I was thrilled, excited, and just couldn't wait to be surprised! Then he called to say he could not give me my surprise because he had to perform for Busta Rhymes's 20th anniversary and it was on my birthday. Oh damn! I asked if he was going to tell me what the surprise was.

He burst out laughing and said, "Mom, I just wanted to spend some time with my girl . . . just you and me in my favorite city. I was taking you to San Diego, so we could walk and talk . . . just you and me . . . like old friends."

My heart opened wide and I teared up a bit. I told him how grateful I was to have him in my life . . . to walk this road as my partner and friend. He was so sweet and so thoughtful . . . my little Leke . . . all grown up surprising his mama. He assured me that he would find a new date as soon as he knew his schedule. San Diego was he and Deisha's favorite city for quick getaways. They had planned a visit there for that coming spring to look at colleges with David and celebrate their wedding anniversary. One month after his death, I traveled to San Diego with my daughter and grandson to look at colleges. Clinging to each other, we watched basketball all night . . . that's what Malik taught us to do.

I Keep Dreaming of My Dead

last night I sat on a concrete plank
with my father and stepmother, Egglon,
they shared stories about their meeting
mostly they shared stories about loving
and co-parenting me
Egglon told me she had a new house
and I was welcomed to come there anytime
I sat listening to their stories
and fell into the white of their teeth

so often now I am dreaming of my dead
Monday it was Aunt Ena
Tuesday it was my mother
Wednesday it was Gerianne
Thursday it was Elma and Ena
Friday it was Roy and Egglon

what messages shall I take from this flight

on cool Brooklyn nights
when the heat ain't working
her mouth is the flambo
lighting my way

I love tribe's new album
We got it from Here . . . Thank You 4 Your Service
Caribbean green avocados
Blue Moon beer

I love *The Low End Theory*
Midnight Marauders   tequila lime chicken
"Bonita Applebum" high-tops

on his second anniversary

I made an altar for my son
       white carnations white sage
       carnelian hearts
       I love Ceni's strong arms around me
       when she breaks out in the most out-of-tune song
       I say *honey, what you say*
       and she says *bae, I'm singing*

       I love my son's cerulean terry robe
       on cool days or hot ones
       I wrap myself and pretend he is hugging me

       I love my mother's voice
       I can still hear her the day I told her my father had died
       how I sobbed and sobbed
       she listened and listened
       then she said
       why yuh crying so daughter
       why I can't understand Cheryl
       and yuh ha yuh mudder
       I am so glad I did not have to tell her about our beloved Leke

Last Words I Said to My Son

"baby I love you
I am so sorry you have to suffer so much
I've always loved you and those little boy pictures
Mami loved your little mischief self
I have a new collage of you near my bed"

"you do?" he asked
"take a screen shot and send it to me Ma
okay I will when I get off the phone"

"I love you"
"love you too Ma"
sistren chuckle . . .

I miss my knight   miss my Phife
I would have preferred to take all his suffering
all his pain so he could stay

I am so grateful for that big love granted me

that's what imma say
when God comes to get me

IV. Funky Diabetic

Funky Diabetic

his voice conjured spells when the notes fell
he could unzip his soul from toes to hairline
praising his hip-hop gods
only James Brown could ride like that

a five-foot assassin snarls freeing da damn microphone

from the deepest corner of his heart
and on his glory day we fastened his Knicks cap like a crown
a sparkling NY jacket unto his baobao shoulders
#5 on his left sleeve
and that boy who once battled killa MCs
rode out to meet his Jesus
a funky diabetic entering his orbit

When Her Child Dies (2)

a mother does not know
that she will be grateful for anything

she will be grateful
that she raised him in church

grateful that he was not killed
in the back of a police cruiser

on the BART London underground NYC subway
grateful he was not killed

by knife gun machete redneck punk
home invasion rope tree trunk

when her child dies
she will be grateful

he did not end up on life support
in hospice care or Rikers Island

she does not know
a street will be named for him in his birth town of Queens

that murals will be painted in Paris Australia South Africa Chicago Trinidad

she will wear his pajamas to bed
cuddle the Minnie Mouse doll he bought at a London airport

and when she finds a gold chain on the sand in South beach
she will know he left it for her because she loves glitter
she will listen to his music over and over
she will tremble at his sass

she will know she is lucky
to still have his songs

she will gather white candles and sage
she will sprinkle white rum and build him an altar

her tears will flow into the Nile
she will give him back to Shango to Oya

she will love herself Ibeji daughter
Ibeji mother more than she ever did before

Malik the Beautiful

Bless the soot of your skin
someday the moon will envy your carnelian eyes
may rain water sprout garnets in your hair
someday I will learn to live without you love
may river sing your songs ever so sweetly
may she keep you company dancing softly side by side .

then
the
lushest
sound
a sequoia
returning

I am Hip-Hop

1 Linden Blvd. Represent, Represent
Tribe Called Quest

2 when a mic is in my grasp
then I'm never hesitant

3 my Favorite Jam in 88'
was Eric B. is president.

4 but now I've returned
but only 2 wreck shop

5 Hip Hop is from the heart
so Quest b' doing shit Non-stop

6 I'm all about the real deal
still no time 4 fakin

7 use soo much french
would swear that I was haitian

8 or Jamaian cuz once in a while
we a fe' chat there's not 2

9 many mc's that can do it like

10 that. Sucker mc's get tanned
from this Trinidad man

11 what's now a 3 man crew in a few
yrs will be aband

12 rippin' shit from state 2 state
land 2 land, so roll out the red

13 carpet cuz here comes the
man.

Phife's Nutshell Lyrics

"Uhm...uhm...

Phife   he   undefeated, unblemished, underrated
Unfiltered, unafraid, unaffected
Undaunted, unabashed, the undeniable
Untouchable, unstoppable, unusual
Underdog
Unsurpassed, unyielding
Unsupportive, fuck you and your feelings
Unrelenting, unscathed, uncontrollable
Unpleasant one, problem with me? Feelin' is mutual
Hah, and that's just me in a nutshell
Uncentered, unchanging, unbreakable
Unconscious, uncouth, unbearable
Unmerciful, unexplainable, unemotional
Uninterested when dealing with unoriginals
Unaccustomed to unproven whack flows
Unresponsive to unapproved stage shows
That's unacceptable, unexciting, lazy fucker
Phife the uncanny, uncommon rhyme spitter

Hah yeah, that's just me in a nutshell
Nutshell, nutshell, nutshell
Said, that's just me in a nutshell
Five Footer in a mothafuckin' nutshell

What? And that's just me in a nutshell
Nutshell, nutshell, nutshell
Ha, Phife Dawg in a nutshell."

You Ibeji Son

You Phife Dawg
You mas camp
You run dis muver boy
You Phife Diggy
You Funky Diabetic
You Don Juice
You Mutty Ranks
You first line ah verse
You big riff

You Diggy Dawg
You home house
You soca-hip-hop
You Ali boxing glove Wop
You 33 LP
You Trini Gladiator
You Rhythm Kids
You Dr Pepper
You fig leaf
You preemie
You we are learning to live without

You Cheryl boo
You mama Ibeji
You peritoneal slugger
You Mt. Pleasant river
You cutlass
You broom
You broad pot spoon
You poui blossom
You pong plantain
You cassava pone
You shekere
You Five-Footer

You Knicks man
You in Claire's with Kaliya
You tossing son in air
You Deisha man
You David poppa san
You Walt main man
You first yu hear meh
You Volta River
You Elegua
You fit my heart

You suck-meh-teeth preacher
You Taiwo firstborn grandson
You of Elma/Ada/JadooMadoo/
Rufus/Roy
You bridge torn down rebuilt
You *Ventilation*
You *Bend Ova*
You machete
You twin
You mama twin

You Cheryl big son
You praise
You chant
You word ONE
You won
You job done
You Phife no drum
You live on
You done flipped da world

Photos

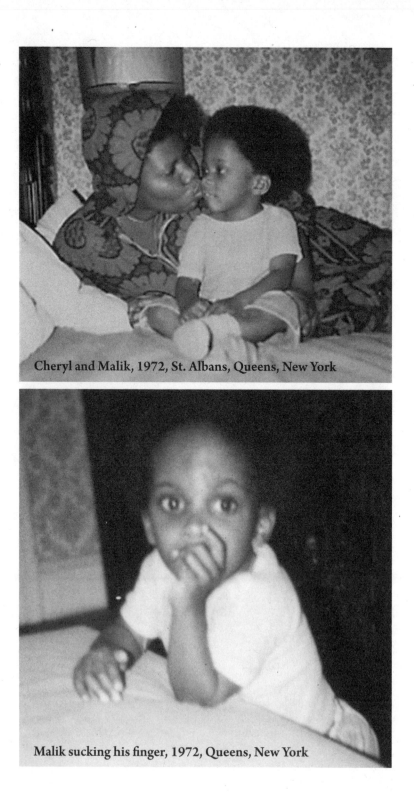

Cheryl and Malik, 1972, St. Albans, Queens, New York

Malik sucking his finger, 1972, Queens, New York

Walt (Malik's dad), Cheryl and Malik,
1973, Queens, New York

Cheryl and Malik,
1973, Queens, New York

Malik at his fourth birthday, 1974, Queens, New York

Phife and Walt at an album release party for *The Low End Theory*, 1991, New York City

Phife in his Atlanta home studio, 1994

Cheryl and Malik on *Lollapalooza Music Tour, A Tribe Called Quest* 1994, Randall's Island, New York

Phife's 2000 LP, *Ventilation*

Phife on da mic at the Bowery Club, New York City, 2003

Phife and Cheryl share the stage at the Bowery Club,
New York City, 2003

Malik and his wife, Deisha, at their wedding in Trinidad and Tobago, 2005

Opposite page: at Malik's wedding, Malik, David (Malik's stepson), Zack (Malik's brother), and Cheryl

Acknowledgments

Special thanks to the editors and journals where these poems first appeared.
Mom Egg Review: "When Her Child Dies"
Mom Egg Review Vox: "He Stood Near My Bed" and "Still the Sweetest Words I Ever Heard"
Like Light: Bright Hill Poets & Writers
Killens Review of Arts & Letters: Gathering at the Waters
Poem-A-Day: "One Long Braid Down She Back"
Black Renaissance Noire: "Apricot Begonias"

Special thanks to the women of Elma's Heart Circle.

I am grateful to Walt Taylor, Aracelis Girmay, Maya Marshall and my Haymarket family, Donna Lee Weber, Malaika Adero, and Irina Linetskaya. And to Sabrina Hayeem-Ladani, Yesenia Montilla and Eric DaSilva, JP Howard, Glenis Redmond, Karole Larsson, Michael and Mark Clemmons, Virginia Alexander and Sheree Renée Thomas. To my grandson David Armstrong, and my grandnieces, Kira and Kaylia. And to Desciana Swinger, my forever love.

Big shout out to Talib Kweli, Ali Shaheed Muhammad, Michael Cirelli, Hanif Abdurraqib, Ana-Maurine Lara, Mahogany L. Browne, Jive Poetic, and Dion Liverpool. And to Marcyliena Morgan and the Harvard Hip-Hop Archives.

Long live A Tribe Called Quest: Phife Dawg, Q-Tip, Jarobi, and Ali!

Creative consultation provided by Donna Lee Weber. Photos courtesy of Marcia Wilson, Deisha Head Taylor, and the Boyce-Taylor family.

Notes

The name Malik means "Master" in Arabic. It also means "King of Kings" and "Angel of God."

In the Nigerian Yoruba tradition twins are known as blessed spirits, or Ibeji. Malik was born with a twin brother named Mikal Boyce. Sadly, his brother only lived for eight hours.

"Phife Dawg" was born Malik Izaak Taylor to Cheryl Boyce-Taylor and Walt Taylor on November 20, 1970, in St. Albans, Queens. He spent most of his early years traveling between New York and Trinidad, his parents' birth home. In the early 90s he cofounded the socially conscious hip-hop group, A Tribe Called Quest. Together, the group changed the face of hip-hop by creating five positive albums which featured Afrocentric lyrics with strong jazz beats and an uplifting message.

It has been very difficult yet healing and enlightening, to write this book about my son, Malik. For weeks after his death, I worried whether or not I had been a good mother to him, and I worried doubly about whether he knew how much I loved him. I don't know where that type of fear comes from. But, after writing this book and recalling our life together, I realize what a big, amazing love we had. I will forever be grateful and thankful that he chose me and that I listened when, at age sixteen, he said, "I'm leaving home, Ma. I'm going to be a rapper."

In this book, I have shared my deep sorrow and ongoing healing about the loss of Malik, better known as Phife Dawg of A Tribe Called Quest. Woven in between the losses are beautiful memories of Malik's childhood and his growth to becoming a hip-hop icon.

This is our story of faith, loss, and renewal.

Biographies

© Dominique Sindayiganza

Cheryl Boyce-Taylor is a poet, workshop facilitator, and founder/curator of Calypso Muse and the Glitter Pomegranate Performance Series. A finalist for the 2018 Paterson Poetry Prize, she earned her MFA in Poetry from Stonecoast: The University of Southern Maine. Cheryl is the author of four collections of poetry: *Raw Air, Night When Moon Follows, Convincing the Body,* and *Arrival,* published in 2017 by Northwestern University Press.

Cheryl was a poetry judge for the Maureen Egan Poetry Prize, the New York Foundation for the Arts and the Astraea Lesbian Foundation for Justice. She has taught poetry workshops for Cave Canem, the New York Public Library, Brooklyn Women of Color Series, JP Howard's Women Writers in Bloom Poetry Salon, Urban Word NYC, *Poets & Writers,* and Poets House.

A Voices of Our Nations Arts fellow, her work has been published in *Prairie Schooner, Poetry, Adrienne, Black Lesbians—We Are the Revolution, Killens Journal of Arts & Letters, Aloud: Voices from the Nuyorican Poets Cafe, Small Axe, Mom Egg Review,* and *Pluck! The Journal of Affrilachian Arts & Culture.*

Her poetry has been commissioned for Ronald K. Brown's EVIDENCE, A Dance Company. Cheryl's work is archived at the Schomburg Center for Research in Black Culture. For more information, visit her website: cherylboycetaylor.net

120 **Malik Izaak Taylor**, best known as Phife Dawg, was a groundbreaking MC and founding member of renowned hip-hop group A Tribe Called Quest. Born and bred in Queens, New York, Malik carried the influence of his parents' Trinidadian culture and his family's propensity toward poetry and storytelling into his singular rhyming verse. (Phife's mother, Cheryl Boyce-Taylor, is a celebrated, published poet, while his grandmother, Eugenia, was celebrated as a skilled storyteller for her church community.) He frequently referred to his home base of Linden Boulevard and 192nd St. in Queens. The intersection was later named Malik "Phife Dawg" Taylor Way in his honor by the City of New York.

Also known as the "Five-Foot Assassin" and "The Five-Footer" (for his 5'3" stature), Phife began ATCQ with high school classmates Q-Tip and Ali Shaheed Muhammad (and for a short time Jarobi White). The group was an integral part of the Native Tongues collective alongside De La Soul, Queen Latifa, and others in early East Coast hip-hop. ATCQ produced a total of seven albums with sales earning gold and/or platinum awards.

Phife collaborated with many other artists on their albums as well. He was featured on songs by De La Soul, Shaquille O'Neal, TLC, Fu-Schnickens, Al Jarreau, Consequence, and Black Eyed Peas. In 2000, Groove Attack Records released Phife's first solo album, *Ventilation: Da LP*. A final solo album titled *Forever* was released in 2020.

As one of their first industry recognitions, ATCQ received the inaugural *Source Magazine* Group of the Year Award in 1994. This was followed by numerous recognitions for their work, including Grammy nominations for Best Rap Album for *Beats, Rhymes and Life* and Best Rap Performance by a Duo or Group for album *1nce Again* in 1997.

In 2005, ATCQ received a Special Achievement Award at the *Billboard* Music Awards and were honorees of VH1's Hip-Hop Honors in 2007. The group was also nominated for a Grammy for Best Long Form Music Video for *Beats, Rhymes & Life: The Travels of A Tribe Called Quest* (2011), Michael Rapaport's documentary about the group.

In 2016, Malik received, alongside his fellow Tribe members, the prestigious ASCAP Golden Note Award. The award was accepted by his mother at the 29th Annual ASCAP Rhythm & Soul Music Awards.

Malik was heralded for weaving sports into his lyrical hip-hop rhymes. Appearing twice on ESPN, Malik also appeared on analytical podcasts of football and basketball games. He acted as Youth Coach to Linden Church of Seventh Day Adventists in Queens, New York, and recruited basketball players for an all-boys school in Connecticut. Phife Dawg is a playable character in the video games NBA 2K7 (2007) and NBA 2K9 (2009). The Knicks presented Malik with his own numbered jersey. He is credited for promoting the use of jerseys in hip-hop performance and identity.

Phife thrived throughout his life despite the challenge of diabetes, naming himself the "Funky Diabetic" and sharing the story of his kidney transplant (given by his wife, Deisha Head Taylor) in the documentary *Beats, Rhymes & Life: The Travels of A Tribe Called Quest*, 2011. His wife and family continue to regularly participate in events supporting diabetes organizations.

Malik died of complications from type 1 diabetes in 2016.

Discography for Phife Dawg

YEAR	ALBUM	LABEL	AWARDED
1990	*People's Instinctive Travels and the Paths of Rhythm* w/ A Tribe Called Quest	Jive, RCA Records	RIAA: Gold
1991	*The Low End Theory* w/ A Tribe Called Quest	Jive	RIAA: Platinum
1993	*Midnight Marauders* w/ A Tribe Called Quest	Jive	RIAA: Platinum
1996	*Beats, Rhymes and Life* w/ A Tribe Called Quest	Jive	RIAA: Platinum MC: Gold
1998	*The Love Movement* w/ A Tribe Called Quest	Jive	RIAA: Gold MC: Gold
2000	*Ventilation*: Da LP—Solo		
2016	*We Got It from Here . . . Thank You 4 Your Service* w/ A Tribe Called Quest	Epic	RIAA: Gold

Also by Cheryl Boyce-Taylor

RAW AIR
NIGHT WHEN MOON FOLLOWS
CONVINCING THE BODY
ARRIVAL